It's Fun To Write

Adventure Stories

Ruth Thomson

SEA-TO-SEA

Mankato Collingwood London

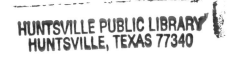

This edition first published in 2013 by
Sea-to-Sea Publications
Distributed by Black Rabbit Books
P.O. Box 3263, Mankato, Minnesota 56002

Printed in the United States of America,
North Mankato, MN.

9 8 7 6 5 4 3

Published by arrangement with the Watts
Publishing Group Ltd, London.

Library of Congress Cataloging-in-Publication Data

Thomson, Ruth, 1949-
 Adventure stories / Ruth Thomson.
   p. cm. -- (It's fun to write)
 ISBN 978-1-59771-405-1 (library binding)
 1. Adventure stories--Authorship--Juvenile literature. 2. Creative writing--
Juvenile literature. I. Title.
 PN3377.5.A37T46 2013
 808.3'87--dc23

                    2011049893

Series Editor: Melanie Palmer
Series Designer: Peter Scoulding
Consultant: Catherine Glavina, Senior Research Fellow, Institute of Education,
University of Warwick, UK.

Acknowledgments:
Cheeky (Saucy) Monkey's Treasure Hunt: illustrations © Lisa Smith;
text © Anne Cassidy. Billy and the Wizard: illustrations © Daniel Howarth;
text © Enid Richemont. Little Joe's Boat Race: illustrations ©Tim Archbold;
text © Andy Blackford. Sinbad and the Whale: illustrations © O'Kif;
text © Martin Waddell. Page 11 (bottom) and page 15, illustrations
© Franklin Watts.

RD/714051/002
December 2012

Contents

About This Book

This book provides engaging ideas to help children develop skills in creative writing and in constructing nonfiction texts. Children need to learn the language, structure, and conventions of different kinds of writing before they can start writing confidently on their own. They need to repeatedly hear and read stories, which they can then talk about, retell, and draw upon to invent their own.

Adventure Stories

The four adventure stories in this book will encourage creativity. They all have fast-paced, action-packed plots, with events that are outside everyday life, involving either a journey (*Little Joe's Boat Race* and *Sinbad and the Whale*), a quest and a chase (*Saucy Monkey's Treasure Hunt*), or righting a wrong (*Billy and the Wizard*).

In common with all adventure stories, the settings start somewhere safe and familiar, such as home or a village. They then move somewhere unfamiliar, dangerous, or forbidding (a stormy sea, woods and hills, a castle, or inside a whale), before returning to safety in the end.

How the Book Works

The book is divided into four chapters. Each one opens with an illustrated adventure story, ideal for sharing and reading out loud.

The stories are followed by a variety of creative writing tasks, such as telling a story from a different point of view, writing a story with a similar structure but different events, making a story map, or retelling a story.

The chapters conclude with story-related nonfiction writing tasks, such as writing lists, directions, recipes, posters, charts, descriptions, or a news report.

Each activity has an example text, clear instructions, "remember" tips, and useful words to enhance writing.

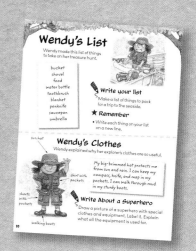

Additional activities can be found on pages 30–31.

Encouraging Writing

Using these adventure stories as springboards offers children a way to write stories without having to invent their own characters or plots. Instead, they could change the problem: What if Sinbad met a giant octopus? They could change the setting: What if Wendy's treasure hunt was set in the jungle? They could change the ending: What if the whale towed Little Joe to the North Pole?

Saucy Monkey's Treasure Hunt

Wendy was going on a treasure hunt. She had a treasure map and all the tools. Then a monkey came along! The monkey carried the tools and the water and the food.

They walked together through the woods. They jumped over the stream. They climbed up the hill.

Wendy found the big rock. She walked ten steps. Wendy found the tree with no leaves. She found a cross on the ground.

The monkey dug a hole. Wendy sat on a rock. The monkey's shovel hit a box. He lifted it up. It was the treasure chest! Wendy and the monkey looked at the treasure. There was a crown. There were gold coins, rings, and necklaces.

Then the monkey picked up the treasure chest. He ran away! Wendy was very angry.

"Come back with my treasure, you bad monkey!" she shouted. But the monkey ran on. He raced down the hill. He jumped over the stream.

"Come back here!" shouted Wendy. The monkey ran into the woods. He rushed through the trees.

He got home and opened the treasure chest, but it was empty! Wendy had all the treasure!

Two Sides to Every Story

The same story can be told from different points of view.
Here is the treasure hunt told from Wendy's point of view.
How do Wendy's feelings change during the story?

The Beginning

I was ready to go on a treasure hunt when a saucy monkey turned up.
I let him pack my bag and carry it for me. I led the way, reading the map,
through the woods, over a stream, and up a hill.

The Middle

I walked ten steps from a big rock and found a cross on the ground.
After all my hard work, I had a rest while the monkey took a long time
to dig a hole. I was thrilled when he found a gleaming box.

The End

We opened the box. It was full of treasure. Suddenly, the saucy monkey
snatched the box and ran away. I was furious and ran after him. The box
was still open, so all the treasure fell out. I got it after all!

✏️ Tell the Saucy Monkey's Tale

Tell the same story from the Saucy Monkey's point of view.
Use the pictures to help you.

The Beginning

The Middle

The End

✏️ Word Match

Choose words
that describe
each picture
the best.

Nouns	Adjectives	Verbs
box	angry	dug
crown	disappointed	opened
hat	empty	packed
hole	excited	ran
jewels	heavy	rested
knapsack	shiny	rushed
shovel	shocked	trudged
treasure	tired	zoomed

Wendy's List

Wendy made this list of things to take on her treasure hunt.

bucket
shovel
food
water bottle
toothbrush
blanket
penknife
saucepan
umbrella

Write Your List

Make a list of things to pack for a trip to the seaside.

★ Remember

• Write each thing on your list on a new line.

Wendy's Clothes

sun hat

Wendy explained why her explorer's clothes are so useful.

My big-brimmed hat protects me from sun and rain. I can keep my compass, knife, and map in my pockets. I can walk through mud in my sturdy boots.

shirt with pockets

shorts with pockets

walking boots

Write About a Superhero

Draw a picture of a superhero with special clothes and equipment. Label it. Explain what all the equipment is used for.

Finding the Way

Wendy followed these directions on her map to find the treasure.

- Go through the woods.
- Cross the stream.
- Climb the hill.
- Find the big rock.
- Walk 10 steps.
- Find the tree with no leaves.
- Look for a cross on the ground.
- Dig for treasure here.

Write Some Directions

Here is a treasure map. Write directions from the starting point, following the trail to the cross that marks where the treasure is buried.

★ Remember

- Use a verb to start each sentence.
- Point out useful landmarks.
- Start a new line each time the route passes a new landmark.
- Keep your sentences short.

Billy and the Wizard

Once there was a wicked wizard. He stole people's food. He took their best things. If anyone complained, he turned them into frogs.

"I can't stand this!" said Billy's mom. "We should do something."

"I have a plan!" said Billy. Billy set off for the wizard's castle.

"Get lost or I'll turn you into something horrible!" shouted the wizard.

"Oh, Mr. Wizard, you're so clever!" sighed Billy.

"I know," replied the wizard.

"You can turn people into frogs," said Billy.

"I can do anything!" boasted the wizard.

"Can you even turn yourself into something?" asked Billy. So the wizard turned into a dragon, breathing fire.

"Wow!" said Billy.

"Can you turn into a horse?"

"Neigh!" replied the wizard.

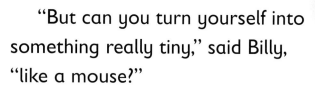

"But can you turn yourself into something really tiny," said Billy, "like a mouse?"

"Squeak!" replied the wizard.

"I bet you can't turn into something really, really tiny," said Billy, "like a fly."

"Buzz!" replied the wizard.

Then Billy swatted the fly with all his might.

"The wicked wizard is gone!" Billy yelled. Lots of the frogs turned back into people and they all had a party to celebrate.

The Wicked Wizard

Write a new story about Billy and the wicked wizard, using the questions below to help you.

Think of a good beginning.

Once upon a time, there was . . .
Long ago, there was . . .
In a castle far away, there lived . . .
A wicked wizard once . . .

What could the wicked wizard do?

He steals children's toys.

He creeps into people's houses.

He writes evil spells.

He turns people into rats.

What could Billy's mom say?
What could Billy say?
Where could Billy go next?

What *big, dangerous* animal could Billy ask the wizard to turn into?

a bear

a lion

a tiger

What *medium-sized* animal could Billy ask the wizard to turn into?

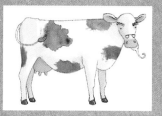
a cow

a donkey

a sheep

a monkey

What *small* animal could Billy ask the wizard to turn into?

a frog

a chicken

a hamster

a tortoise

What *tiny* animal could Billy ask the wizard to turn into?

a worm

a mosquito

a beetle

a wasp

What could Billy do next? Use an interesting verb for the end of the story.

Verbs

crushed
squashed
squished
squeezed
smashed

15

The Wizard's Recipe Book

The wizard had a big book of secret recipes for making magic potions. Here is his recipe for taming dragons. Notice how it is laid out.

Things you need, listed in the order of their use

The title of the recipe

A POTION FOR TAMING DRAGONS

Ingredients
1 rotten boiled egg
A handful of dust
2 rats' tails
4 caterpillars
A cup of moldy bread crumbs
6 rose thorns
10 toenail clippings

Instructions
1. Mash the egg with the dust.
2. Cut the rats' tails into thin slices and stir them into the mixture.
3. Squash the caterpillars and add them to the mixture.
4. Whisk in the bread crumbs.
5. Sprinkle the thorns and nail clippings on top.
6. Boil the mixture until it bubbles and then let it cool.

Feed the potion cold to angry dragons.

Numbered steps

Amount of each ingredient

Extra information

Write a Recipe

Write your own recipe for a magic potion.

★ Remember

- Give your recipe a title. List some disgusting ingredients, saying how much you need of each one.
- Write the instructions in steps. Say what to do first, then next, and so on.
- Use a verb to start each sentence.
- Number each step.
- Add any extra information.

Verbs

add
bake
boil
chop
crush
cut
fill

fry
measure
mix
pour
roast
swirl
thicken

A "Wanted!" poster

A big bold title

Imagine that the villagers have made a "Wanted!" poster of the wicked wizard. It might look like this.

The person's name and the reason he or she is wanted

A description of the person

The reward in big letters

WANTED!
The wicked wizard for stealing food

A picture showing what the person looks like

The wizard has white hair and a long white beard. He has mean eyes, a big nose, and wears a long blue gown and hat.

REWARD $1,000

Make a Poster

Make your own "Wanted!" poster of a nasty character, such as a witch, a robber, or a pirate.

★ Remember

When you make a "Wanted!" poster:
- Start with a big title.
- Write the name of the wanted person and the reason he or she is wanted.
- Draw a picture of the person.
- Write a description of what he or she looks like.
- Offer a large reward.

Word Bank

bent
bushy
cruel
eyebrows
glasses
hunched
mustache
pointed
skinny
sly
warty

Little Joe's Boat Race

It was the day of the Village Boat Race. Little Joe took his boat along. The other boys laughed at him.

"Your boat's MUCH too small, Little Joe! And so are YOU!"

Little Joe sat by the river and watched the race. The biggest boat started to drift toward the rocks.

"Help, Little Joe!" cried its owner.

Only Little Joe was light enough to climb on the branch and reach the boat.

Then he fell! He landed on the boat as it raced toward the rapids!

Little Joe managed to steer the boat between the rocks.

A swan thought he was trying to steal her eggs. She tried to peck him.

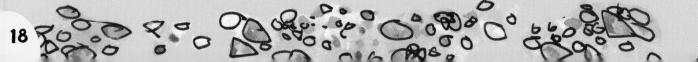

After a while, the river reached the sea. The sky turned black.

First it began to rain. Then it hailed.

Little Joe saw a huge whale. It was stuck on the rocks. Little Joe raced to the rescue.

He threw a rope to the whale and pulled it off the rocks.

Then the wind dropped and the boat stopped moving. But the whale pulled Little Joe and the boat toward home.

A big crowd was waiting on the shore to cheer him. The boys from the village were there, too.

"Well done, Little Joe!" they cried.
"You're the best sailor in the whole village!"

Little Joe's Story Map

Tell the story of Little Joe's adventure, following his route on this story map.

The Start

village

river

rapids

swan's nest

rocks

sea

The End

port

shore

Make a Story Map

Draw a story map to plan a new adventure about Little Joe.

The start: Where could Little Joe start?

house   village   riverbank   field

Where could he sail his boat—first, next, and finally?

through rapids   under a bridge   past rowboats   out to sea

What happens to Little Joe at sea?

ship   seagulls   storm   rocks

The end: How will Little Joe get home? What happens in the end?

sailors   crowd   flags   clap   prize

Now write your story, using your story map to help you.

What's the Weather Like?

Little Joe made a book describing the weather on his journey.

Make a Book

Make your own book showing what the weather is like every day for a week.

★ Remember

- Write a big title for your book.
- Draw a cover.
- Write the day of the week in big letters on every page.
- Write a word that best describes the weather every day.
- Draw your own pictures for sunshine, clouds, rain, hail, snow, and fog.

LITTLE JOE'S WEATHER BOOK

Monday	breezy	
Tuesday	rainy	
Wednesday	hail	
Thursday	stormy	
Friday	sunny	
Saturday	cloudy	
Sunday	cold	

There are all kinds of other words you could use instead of *rainy*, such as drizzly, pouring, showery, spitting, teeming, or wet.

What other words could you use instead of *windy*, *cold*, or *sunny*?

Word Bank

bright
foggy
freezing
frosty
icy

misty
rainy
snowy
thundery
windy

Which Boat is This?

Here is a description of one of the boats in this picture. Can you tell which one it is?

This boat has a wooden hull. It has three different-sized masts. Each one has a flag on the top. The sails are rolled up. Pirates once sailed in ships like these.

Describe a Boat

Draw a picture of another boat. Write a few sentences describing it.

★ Remember

When you describe an object, write about:
- what it looks like—its shape, size, and color
- its different parts.

flags

mast

sail

tiller

cabin

hull

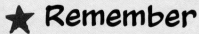

Sinbad and the Whale

Sinbad the Sailor made pots of money on his first voyage to sea. On the way home, his ship sailed by a beautiful, low-lying island.

"Yippee!" cheered the crew as they landed. "We'll hold a We're-Rich-Now party in honor of Sinbad the Sailor."

Sinbad felt uneasy.

"There's something fishy about this place!" he warned his friend Ali. But Ali was too busy to listen. He lit the fire for the barbecue and the island woke up! It lashed its huge tail, and it moved!

"Oh no!" gasped Sinbad. "This island is a whale!"

WOOOOOOOOSH!

They all ended up in the sea. The whale swallowed Ali and Sinbad the Sailor. The rest of the crew swam back to the ship and sadly sailed home.

Deep, deep down inside the whale, Ali and Sinbad were swimming in stinky water. There were small crabs and huge jellyfish and broken palm trees.

"How do we get out of this?" groaned Ali.

"Think, think, THINK!" Sinbad said. And he thought and he thought.

"It's whale tickle time!" laughed Sinbad. Sinbad grabbed a palm tree,

stripped off the palms and handed Ali the trunk. Then Sinbad swam to the whale's throat. He tickled and tickled and tickled until the whale began to cough. **YARRRGGGHHH!**

"Now!" yelled Sinbad. "Here we go!" **WOOOOOOOOSH!**

They were out of the whale, but lost at sea, bobbing around on a broken palm tree!

"What now?" sighed Ali.

"Leave it to me!" said Sinbad. He knew how to steer by the stars so they set off for home. The palm tree sailed into harbor. The ship was there with all of Sinbad's money.

"You're back!" cried the crew. "We thought we'd lost you!" Then Sinbad, Ali, and the crew had their We're-Rich-Now party . . . but not on the whale!

Sinbad's Adventure

Retell the story of Sinbad as a conversation between Sinbad and his sailors.

1. What do the sailors say when they land on the island?

2. What does Sinbad say about the island?

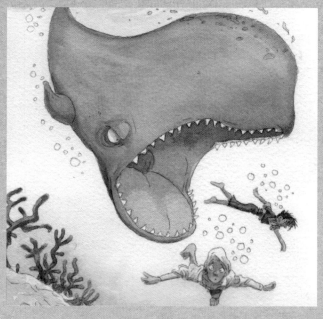

3. What do Sinbad and the sailors say when the island suddenly moves?

4. What do Sinbad and Ali say when the whale swallows them?

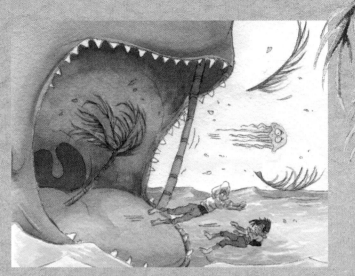

5. What does Sinbad tell Ali to do?

6. What does Sinbad say next?

7. What do Sinbad and Ali say on their way home?

8. What do the sailors say when Sinbad and Ali arrive?

9. What might Sinbad say at the party?

Sinbad's Story

If Sinbad's story was reported in a newspaper, it might read like this. Notice the way the story is written and how it is laid out.

A bold headline

The writer's name

Who the story is about

When it took place

Where it took place

What happened

The words of the person

Sinbad saved from Whale

by Iva Goodstory

A well-known sailor has told of his lucky escape from inside a whale last week—by tickling its throat with palm leaves so it coughed him out.

Sinbad said he and his crew were about to have a party on an island in the Atlantic Ocean, when the island suddenly started to move. "That's when I realized it was a whale," said the 30-year-old.

Seconds later, Sinbad and his crew were tossed into the sea and had to swim for their lives.

The huge whale swallowed Sinbad and his friend, Ali. "We were terrified," said Sinbad. "It was dark and stinky inside the whale. We had to find a way out."

A crowd cheered Sinbad

The whale dived back into the ocean after Sinbad had escaped.

An expert sailor, Sinbad used the stars to find his way home. A huge crowd greeted him on his return.

"We thought he had gone forever," said one of his crew, "so we were very happy to see him again."

Sinbad has faced many alarming moments at sea, but declared, "This was the worst!"

A caption about the picture

A comment that sums up the story

Write a News Report

Imagine that you have interviewed one of Sinbad's crew for a newspaper. Write a news report about his experience.

★ Remember
- Start with a big, bold headline.
- Add your name as the writer.
- Write short paragraphs, saying:
    - who the story is about
    - when it took place
    - where it took place
    - what happened in order.
- Draw a picture and write a caption about the story.
- Make a final comment.

Useful Words

barbecue	hauled
calm	hurled
captain	journey
celebrated	massive
flung	splashed

Other Adjectives for Scared

alarmed	
afraid	horrified
dismayed	shaken
frightened	startled
	worried

More Writing Ideas

Amazing Adjectives

Describe the Saucy Monkey using different
letters of the alphabet, e.g. an **a**nnoying
monkey, a **b**ossy monkey, and so on.

Noun Nonsense

Choose an extract from one of the stories.

Change every noun in it to completely change the story or to create wonderful
nonsense. For example, you could change this extract ... They walked through *the
woods.* They jumped over *the stream.* They climbed up *the hill.* Wendy found *the
big rock.* She walked ten *steps.* Wendy found *the tree with no leaves.* She looked
at the ground ... into something with a completely different setting and action:
They walked through *the shopping mall.* They jumped over *the fence.* They
climbed up *the stairs.* Wendy found *the big picnic area.* She walked ten *paces.*
Wendy found *the café with no one waiting in line.* She looked at *the menu.*

Splendid Sentences

Choose a simple sentence from one of the stories, such as Billy set off for
the wizard's castle. Think of ways to enrich it.

Vary the verb: Billy *started out* for the wizard's castle.

Change words: Billy *climbed the steep hill* to the wizard's *cave.*

Add extra words: Billy *set off at top speed* for the *horrible* wizard's
gloomy castle.

Add words at the beginning: *The very next morning*, Billy set off for the
wizard's castle.

Add words at the end: Billy set off for the wizard's castle, *perched high
on a distant hill*.

Add a simile: *As brave as a lion*, Billy set off for the wizard's castle.

Use alliteration: Billy **b**oldly **b**ounded **b**etween **b**oulders.

Below are some additional writing activities related to each story.

Saucy Monkey's Treasure Hunt
- Make two word lists of verbs and adjectives, contrasting the different ways that Wendy and the Saucy Monkey move.
- Draw your own treasure map. Include labeled landmarks for treasure hunters.
- Think of adjectives to describe items of treasure—a crown, a chain, coins, a necklace, a ring, jewels, a bracelet.
- Write an exciting adventure about a treasure hunt. It could be about a band of pirates, a gang of thieves, or a bunch of children.

Billy and the Wizard
- Make an illustrated word book contrasting different words for big and small, for example, a huge elephant and a tiny mouse.
- Tell the story from the wizard's point of view. Imagine how he feels when Billy knocks on his door.
- Imagine what would have happened if the wizard had turned into bigger and bigger animals instead of smaller and smaller ones. What would Billy have done to trick him?

Little Joe's Boat Race
- Imagine you are one of Joe's friends. Think of questions you might ask him when he returns home. Use the question words: *Who? What? Where? When? How? Why?*
- Make a weather thesaurus. Divide a piece of paper into four columns with these headings: **Sunny   Rainy   Windy   Cloudy**.
  Make a list of as many different alternative words as you can.
- Write a description of the places that Joe passes on his journey to the sea.

Sinbad and the Whale
- Find out some facts about blue whales and write a report about them.
- The story says Sinbad made lots of money on his voyage. Imagine how he made this money and write a story about it.
- Write a menu for the feast that the sailors gave Sinbad and Ali on their return.

Grammar Glossary

Nouns

A noun is the name of a person, an animal, an object, or a place.

a person	an animal	an object	a place
a boy	a frog	a boat	a castle

A proper noun is the name of a particular person or place. A proper noun always begins with a capital letter.

a person	a place
Billy	The Old Lighthouse

Adjectives

An adjective gives more information about a noun. Here are some examples:

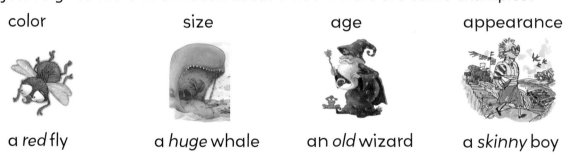

color	size	age	appearance
a *red* fly	a *huge* whale	an *old* wizard	a *skinny* boy

Verbs

A verb is an action word. It describes what is happening in a sentence.

The whale *swallowed* Ali and Sinbad.

Little Joe *sat* by the river and *watched* the race.

The monkey *dug* a hole.